WOOD PASTURE

Acknowledgements:

Author: Roland Stiven - the author acknowledges considerable input from Peter Quelch, Mike Smith, Kate Holl and Helen Gray. Information on selected veteran trees was provided by Donald Rodger.

Photography:

Jane Begg front cover, 15, 20, 24, 31, **Sandy Coppins** 10 top right, 17 bottom left, 19, 23 bottom right, 33, **Niall Corbett** 21 top left, 21 main pic, 36, **Lorne Gill/SNH** 7, 10 top left, 17 top left, 22 bottom left & bottom right, 23 bottom left, 26, 28, **Frank Greenaway** 17 bottom right, **Kate Holl** front cover, 2, 3, 4, 5, 9, 10 bottom right, 23 top & middle, 24 bottom, 27 bottom, **Roger Key** 21 bottom left, 25, **Iain MacGowan** 10 top middle, **Robin Miller** 30, **Natural History Society of Glasgow** 27 top, **Peter Quelch** front cover, title page, contents page, 11, 22 top right, 34, 35, back cover, **Veteran Tree Initiative** 8, 18

Illustration:

Jaqueline Stevenson 29, 32

National Gallery of Scotland, Edinburgh 12

Scottish Natural Heritage

Design and Publications

Battleby

Redgorton

Perth PH1 3EW

Tel: 01738 444177

Fax: 01738 458613

E-mail: pubs@rsnh.gov.uk

www.snh.org.uk

Cover images:

Medieval oakwood wood pasture at Cadzow, Lochwood SSSI, Cattle grazing in wood pasture

Back page image:

Rowan 'Bird Tree' growing inside veteran alder tree, Glen Finglas

WOOD PASTURE

by

Roland Stiven and Kate Holl

Foreword

Woods, beasts and people have been inextricably linked in the Scottish past since prehistoric times. Five thousand years ago, the woods covered half the land surface, perhaps more. Animals grazed within and around them, and men hunted the animals. As farming developed, people kept their domesticated beasts in the woods as well as on the pastures, a practice that continued even when the woods themselves became relatively scarce and agricultural crops covered most of the ground available. At one time, not so long ago, every wood in Scotland was still being used for grazing and shelter as well as for wood produce. The balance between the two forms of utilisation was hard to strike: too much grazing, and the wood would gradually disappear; too little, and the herbage would be shaded out.

The subtle knowledge of how to manage this process well disappeared in the agricultural revolution of the late eighteenth and early nineteenth centuries. At this point, mixed land use was replaced almost everywhere by division into two categories. Woods with grass in them were permanently enclosed and used for timber production or for sport, so they grew thicker and darker. Pastures with trees on them were treated as any other pasture, and if the woods vanished under the pressure, that hardly mattered as after 1850 timber could be bought for farm work at the nearest railhead. We were largely left with the alternatives of dense enclosed woods or overgrazed open ones.

Such ancient wood pastures as remain to us are precious remnants. As well as being valuable habitats for a great range of animals, insects and plants, they speak to us of human history. They often contain within their bounds veteran trees of great age, symbols of longevity and subjects of legend. They tell us how land was once managed for multipurpose use. With their openings, their glades and their encrusted, twisted trees, they make a dappled world magical and old. Unfortunately, they are also largely unprotected by modern legislation. Because the tree canopy may occupy less than 20% of the airspace above them, they often do not come under forestry rules governing felling and planting. Because they are not man-made ruins or buildings, they are not ever protected as antiquities.

Nevertheless they are as much evidence of our past as a castle ruin or long barrow, and as valuable to our natural heritage as many a famous forest.

This excellent booklet explains all this, and invites us to know them better. To visit the Cadzow oaks is to stand amongst a group of medieval beings, mature long before Mary, Queen of Scots, and John Knox were even conceived. To visit Glen Finglas in the autumn, when the hazels are laden with nuts and the fieldfares are busy in the rowans, is to visit a scene unchanged in essence since the servants of the Stewart kings rode through, driving the stags into the deer traps at the foot of the glen. These are old cultural landscapes of a rarity and beauty we cannot replicate or easily replace.

But here we are also asked not only to appreciate and protect wood pasture, but to rise to the challenge of renewing it and extending it. Less than 17,000 hectares of wood pasture remains. The greatest enemy of its future is ignorance of its importance, but its management is a problem even for owners who appreciate it, since it remains hard to rediscover the techniques for keeping trees and herbage in balance. Yet, with a will, the life of a wood pasture can be renewed and extended by methods explained here. Even more importantly, a glimpse is shown of how new wood pastures could be a land use for the future. Though they cannot instantly acquire the biodiversity and cultural patina of the ancient wood pastures, they could be a way of reconciling farming and forestry, and are more likely, because wood pasture is so attractive, to win public approval than either a change to dense forestry or to bare sheep run. At a time when we are likely to see big changes in upland land use, it is exciting to see a lesson from history put to modern use.

Chris Smout

Chris Smout
Historiographer Royal in Scotland

Contents

Loch Wood SSSI

Above: a pollarded veteran ash tree grows on boulders cleared long ago from terraces in Rassal Ashwood

Opposite page: many wood pastures contain the ruins of agricultural buildings and homesteads, evidence of man's historical occupation which has created this biocultural landscape

Widely distributed throughout upland and lowland Scotland, wood pastures are the living remnants of a historic land management system. This habitat is a type of very open woodland; it is a cross between woodland and grassland, or sometimes woodland and heathland.

Grazing animals are, and always have been, part and parcel of the wood pasture system which is a habitat maintained by grazing, just like the old flower-rich hay meadows. This system has not only provided valuable sheltered grazing pasture for centuries, but has also satisfied the needs of generations of communities for tree products, including firewood and leaves for forage. The trees may therefore show signs of previous management. In the lowlands, the habitat is a product of the historic management of medieval forests, parks or designed landscapes associated with large houses.

Wood pastures are a kind of living ancient monument, where the living things - the ancient trees - are of as much interest as built structures and earthworks which may exist elsewhere, for they are part of our man-made or cultural landscape.

Until very recently this habitat was presumed to be confined to the lowlands, but survey work has shown that wood pasture is in fact widely distributed throughout Scotland, with an estimated extent of between 8,000 and 17,000 hectares. To reflect its international importance and vulnerability, as well as its value for a wide range of associated priority species, and its role in representing the historical legacy of past management, wood pasture and parkland has been made the subject of a priority Habitat Action Plan where a range of measures to protect and enhance this precious and important habitat have been specified.

What is wood pasture?

Wood pasture is a landscape of scattered trees in a grassland or heathland setting. It is a habitat fashioned by generations of rural people grazing livestock and maintaining trees on the same site. To create wood pasture the grazing needed to be just right: light enough to allow trees to grow (and occasionally to regenerate), but sufficient to prevent a woodland forming and shading out the pasture. Where this was achieved over a long period of time, a unique habitat has developed which today harbours many rare and important species.

Ancient wood pasture includes the parklands and designed landscapes of big estates such as Dalkeith or Drummond, the vestiges of royal and noble hunting forests such as Cadzow and Glen Finglas, and a range of smaller sites that perhaps survived through the vagaries of chance and circumstance.

Why is it important?

The defining feature of ancient wood pasture is the presence of veteran trees often many centuries old. They can be very big and may show signs of having been cut back in the past. Veteran trees often host long-established communities of fungi, lichens and specialist insects and are also home to birds, bats and other wildlife. Trees like this, surrounded by open semi-natural grassland and nectar-filled wild flowers create a special wildlife habitat and a classic landscape.

The rural practices that created and maintained wood pasture have all but died out, overtaken by modern livestock farms and forestry plantations. However, the wood pasture that remains provides evidence of a land-use tradition practised for centuries throughout the uplands and lowlands of Scotland.

Interest in wood pasture habitats in Scotland is very recent and we still have much to learn. Most importantly we need to be able to distinguish between overgrazed native woodland that needs protection, and wood pasture habitat of value where grazing would improve biodiversity. Many of our native woodlands are grazed by livestock, rabbits and deer, often to the point of destruction, so both foresters and nature conservationists are generally wary of keeping livestock in woods. However, combining grazing and woodland under wood pasture may offer benefits to farming and other users of the countryside.

Deadwood - whether fallen or standing - provides an important habitat for the specialist insects associated with these ancient wood pastures

Over the hill?

When you begin to look, you can find veteran trees throughout Scotland: in churchyards, gardens, ancient woodlands, field boundaries and in the remaining areas of parkland and wood pasture. It is difficult to define precisely what constitutes a veteran tree, but the general characteristics are easily appreciated.

Veteran trees are old. Many have been standing for hundreds of years; a few can mark a millennium, and the odd yew might even predate Christianity. Old, however, can be a relative term. Willows or birches start getting old when they are 60 or 70 (although some may become much older), whereas a 200-year-old oak will only just be reaching its prime. Besides, it is not always easy to estimate the age of a tree unless there are records of its early existence.

Size can be an indicator but, again, it varies by species and by circumstance.

Some veteran trees are big. The King of the Woods in Jedburgh is an oak some seven metres in girth and the Fortingall Yew spreads out in a hollow ring over 16 metres around. Veteran hawthorns, however, may be barely a few metres tall.

A veteran oak at Cadzow. It is often hard to age trees such as this accurately. Some of the Cadzow oaks have been dated by dendrochronology to 1444, and the local legend that the trees were originally planted by David I in the twelfth century may be true

Some well-known examples of veteran trees in Scotland

1. **The Birnam Oak.**

   This majestic old veteran stands on the banks of the River Tay near the Perthshire village which gives the tree its name. With an impressive trunk girth of 5 metres and long, spreading limbs, it is reputed to be a surviving remnant of Birnam Wood, immortalised by Shakespeare in *Macbeth*.

2. **The Capon Oak.**

   With a vast trunk diameter of 10 metres, this spectacular old veteran has split and decayed, and now relies on a system of timber props for support. A survivor of the once extensive Jed Forest which clothed the Teviot Valley in centuries past, it possibly got its name because rents in kind (including capons) were rendered to the landowner under it. Located next to the A68 a few miles south of Jedburgh.

3. **The Newbattle Abbey Sycamore.**

   Sycamore has long been naturalised in Scotland and has the capacity to live to a great age. The sycamore with the oldest known planting date (1550) in Scotland is the handsome, open-grown tree which graces the frontage to Newbattle Abbey, near Dalkeith. Over 450 years it has attained a trunk girth of 5 metres and height of 26 metres.

4. **The 'King Tree'.**

   Sweet chestnut was thought to have been introduced to Britain by the Romans. It is a species capable of attaining great age and several old veterans can be found throughout Scotland. One of the biggest stands within a housing estate in the Stirlingshire town of Denny. Known locally as the 'King Tree', it boasts an impressive trunk girth of 8 metres and is probably in the region of 450 years old.

5. **Queen Mary's Thorn.**

   Trees don't have to be huge to be veterans. The venerable old hawthorn which graces the quadrangle of St Mary's College of St Andrews University is said to have been planted by Mary, Queen of Scots, around 1563, on one of her many visits to the town. This legendary link with one of Scotland's most famous historical figures continues to survive by the production of new and vigorous growth.

6. **The Fortingall Yew.**

   Nestling in the churchyard of the picturesque village of Fortingall stands a unique yew tree. Yews are renowned for their great longevity and slow rate of growth, and this yew tree is thought by some to be in the region of 3,000 years old, making it arguably the oldest living organism in Europe. All that survives of a tree once measured as 17 metres in girth in 1769 are two remnants now enclosed within a stone wall.

7. **The Great Yew of Ormiston.**

   Scotland is home to several remarkable ancient yews, the outer branches of which have fallen to ground level and layered, thereby enclosing the mother tree in a dense ring of foliage. A prime example of this growth form can be seen in the remarkable layered yew at Ormiston Hall, in East Lothian. The superb central trunk measures 7 metres in girth and stands centre stage in the middle of an open, central cavern formed by the ever-spreading outer ring of foliage. Legend tells that the religious reformer John Knox preached under the shade of the great yew in the sixteenth century.

8. **'The King of the Forest'.**

   A majestic Scots pine known locally as 'The King of the Forest' stands proudly within Muirward Wood, near Scone. This has the largest girthed trunk so far recorded for this species at 6 metres, and with its equally impressive height of 31 metres it exerts a dominant presence over the surrounding younger plantation. A remarkable example of this species.

9. **The Glen Lyon Ash.**

   Tucked midway up a beautiful Perthshire glen stands an ancient ash tree of exceptional proportions. Its trunk measures 6 metres in girth and it once exceeded 30 metres in height until it was recently re-pollarded. Possibly in the region of 400 - 500 years in age, this is an exceptional example of a species not renowned for its longevity. The truncated stump is rapidly pushing out new vigorous growth, which should ensure the tree's survival for another century or two.

10. **The 'Act of Union' Beech Trees.**

    Clinging on for dear life to the wind-swept slopes of North Berwick Law stand a group of beech trees which were planted to commemorate the Act of Union between the Scottish and English Parliaments in 1707. A species widely planted in Scotland for many centuries, few live much longer than 300 years and the North Berwick trees are some of the oldest in Scotland.

Further remarkable examples of veteran trees in Scotland may be found in *Heritage Trees of Scotland*.

Technically, a tree becomes 'ancient' when the annual growth increment starts to decline. Although the tree's growth rings may get narrower as its girth increases, there comes a point when the actual volume of new wood created each year starts to decrease. This tends to be associated with a reduction of the canopy, the death and loss of branches and the advance of decay fungi which hollow out the heartwood and the broken stumps of branches. This period of 'retrenchment' may last for decades or even centuries while the tree decays and maintains a sparse living crown.

The Birnam Oak

The Fortingall Yew in 1826, by Strutt, 1826

Diagram to show some of the types of veteran tree

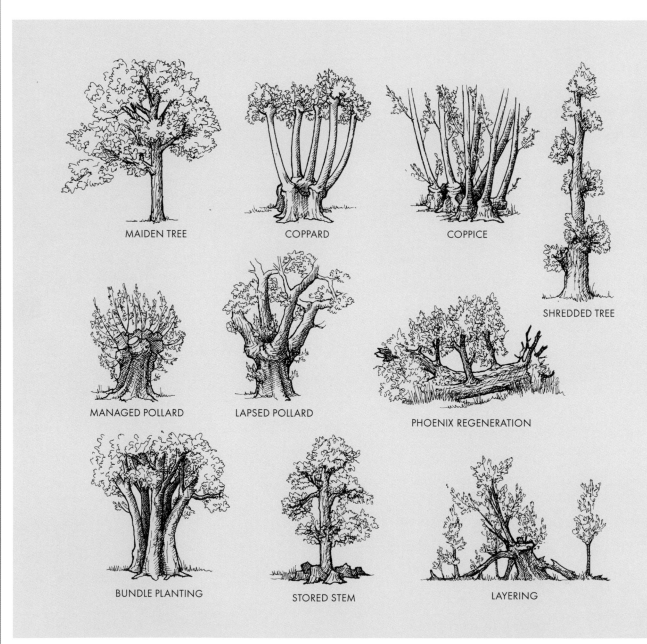

MAIDEN TREE

COPPARD

COPPICE

SHREDDED TREE

MANAGED POLLARD

LAPSED POLLARD

PHOENIX REGENERATION

BUNDLE PLANTING

STORED STEM

LAYERING

Signs from the past

Inevitably many trees that have been around for a long time show signs of less natural wear and tear, having been pruned or cut back at some point in their history. Some were felled and have re-grown again from the stump as multi-stemmed trees. Broadleaved woods were often repeatedly coppiced like this to produce smaller dimension poles, fuelwood or charcoal.   Oak trees in the west of Scotland, for example, were coppiced for various periods throughout the last few centuries. Their bark was in demand for tanning and the wood for charcoal for iron smelting.

If the land was grazed, the trees were often pollarded, (cut above the level of grazing animals). Pollard regrowth was periodically cut back possibly to provide animal feed, poles or firewood. Many veteran trees show signs of coppicing or pollarding and, paradoxically, it may have been these interventions which contributed to their longevity. Regular pollarding produces a wide-girthed short tree, less prone to being blown down, difficult to fell and often unsuitable for timber.

The regular practice of pollarding trees died out at least a hundred years ago in rural Scotland and many veterans now show the multiple large-stemmed form typical of lapsed pollards or hedgerow trees left to grow on.

A lapsed veteran ash pollard in Glen Finglas

Veteran coppiced oak near Loch Sunart

9

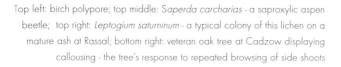

Top left: birch polypore; top middle: *Saperda carcharias* - a saproxylic aspen beetle; top right: *Leptogium saturninum* - a typical colony of this lichen on a mature ash at Rassal; bottom right: veteran oak tree at Cadzow displaying callousing - the tree's response to repeated browsing of side shoots

Scarred for life

The tree may be losing vitality in its old age, but this is the period when it starts becoming more interesting to other forms of life: a self-renewing deadwood resource playing host to an ever richer and more diverse flora and fauna. Bats and birds move in to crevices and holes, and fungi start softening up the deadwood, releasing nutrients for other fungi and for insects. Mosses, ferns, bryophytes and even other tree seedlings ('Bird Trees') take hold in water-filled forks, and over time a rich lichen flora can develop, some species being particular to open-grown trees. Fungi and mycorrhizae in and around the roots also often develop into complex and interesting communities over the lifetime of the tree.

Deadwood or saproxylic insects are a special feature of veteran trees, with many threatened, rare and uncommon beetles, moths and flies relying on them for a home. Some species have strict habitat requirements, colonising only lightning strikes, sap runs or old wounds. Groups of veteran trees, as found in parklands, old orchards or wood pasture, are more likely to possess a range of micro-habitats and thereby develop a broad biodiversity interest.

As time goes by...

It is not just flora and fauna that grow alongside the veteran trees. People are naturally drawn to them. We are awed by their size. We derive a sense of wonder from their timelessness and tenacity and we admire their rough beauty. In the past, some species, such as yew, oak and rowan, were held sacred. Rowan was often planted outside homes to ward off evil spirits. Still today, many people find old trees spiritually uplifting and recognise in them a connection to the earth which is missing from much of modern life.

Veteran trees are often linked to legends or folklore. It is said that Pontius Pilate played within the Yew at Fortingall when his father was stationed at a Roman garrison there. The Fraser Yew in Stratherrick was the gathering point of the Fraser clan when rallied to battle. The twin hawthorns at the now abandoned village of Polwarth in Berwickshire have been danced around at village weddings since the fifteenth century although it is unlikely that the present trees are the originals. In Melrose there is even a stone marking the site of the 'Eildon Tree' where, according to legend, Thomas the Rhymer, the Border poet, met the Queen of the Fairies.

Veteran trees inevitably become features in the landscape, witnessing history, marking time and holding sway over the generations of people and communities who come and go. They are living monuments to our heritage, often acting as guides to previous landscapes: showing the lines of old roads and field boundaries, where the river used to run or the graveyard once was. Although the practical uses of the trees - for shelter, fodder or as boundary markers - may no longer be important their cultural, spiritual, aesthetic and historic significance increases.

A dying race...

Surprisingly, given the more impressive forests of many European countries, the UK holds an internationally important resource of veteran trees. Despite this, too many are still being lost: to agricultural intensification, to afforestation, to the development of new roads and housing, from disease (such as Dutch elm disease) and through simple disregard and neglect. The emphasis placed today on safety and landowner's liability has also resulted in the felling of old trees in public places with little consideration given to their inherent value, or to possible alternatives to their removal.

However, the main threat to the overall resource is the lack of replacements to the veteran generation. We are living off a legacy from the past that we have failed to maintain. In losing the trees we also lose the specialised wildlife: the bats, craneflies, stag beetles, leafy lichens and the weird and wonderful fungi. If these species are to survive, they need a steady supply of 'new veterans' and some deliberate management to keep existing veteran trees alive in the meantime.

A lovely old veteran birch with rot hole in a wood pasture near Fort Augustus

Wood pasture: a veteran habitat

Origins of wood pasture

How did wood pastures come into being? In the lowlands, stands of open-grown trees were deliberately created to provide sheltered grazing for stock. In some cases the trees were planted together with introduced ornamental species such as horse chestnut and sweet (Spanish) chestnut, both of which are common in parkland sites. The oldest of the oaks at Cadzow, near Glasgow, was reputedly planted by King David I in the twelfth century.

Wood pasture trees in the uplands are more likely to be descendants of the post-glacial natural woodland. The process of opening the woodland canopy will have started with wild herbivores such as elk, deer, cattle and boar, and the burning of glades by early peoples to favour pasture and hunting. Since then cattle, sheep, pigs, goats and ponies have been grazed throughout upland Scotland. Raising black (Highland) cattle and sheep for sale to lowland graziers was a mainstay of the upland rural economy prior to the clearances. Families would move to the hill shielings with their animals for the summer grazing, and drive them to market in the autumn. This seasonal grazing would provide good conditions for the development and continuation of wood pasture.

Design or default?

Were the trees deliberately looked after, or did they survive by chance, regenerating occasionally when grazing pressure dropped? There was probably wide variation depending on circumstance. The hunting forests, which often incorporated wood pasture, were closely protected. Many surviving sites, including Dalkeith, Glen Finglas, Drummond and Glen Artney, can be traced back to such a past. The formal parklands and designed landscapes from the sixteenth to the nineteenth century may have been superimposed on areas that were previously simple wood pasture, keeping some of the big mature trees and adding other landscape features as fashions changed.

However, the trees were valued for more than just aesthetics or shelter. People needed firewood, charcoal, fencepoles, timber, tar, rosin and wild honey. Branches were possibly also lopped for leaf fodder or to let the animals strip the bark in the winter. Enclosed woodlands were mostly privately owned, so trees on the open grazings may have been all that was available to the majority of people.

The sheep farming of the last two centuries and continuing high deer numbers must have tipped the balance for many upland wood pastures. Persistent year-round grazing together with the decline of subsistence uses have resulted in centuries-old wood pastures being neglected and lost. Those that remain retain the more tenacious tree species such as alder, oak and hawthorn.

View of Bothwell Castle (1814). Hugh William Williams depicts cattle being driven to market: the woods were seasonally grazed by livestock

Until recently, interest in wood pasture focused on lowland sites particularly in England and Wales. There are a few lowland sites in Scotland such as Dalkeith, Cadzow, Lochwood and Glenlee in Dumfries and Galloway which are designated as Sites of Special Scientific Interest for their insects and lichens. Other parkland sites are known through the Inventory of Gardens and Designed Landscapes in Scotland. In 1997, the Woodland Trust purchased Glen Finglas, and gradually, as its wood pasture status became apparent, a wider interest in upland wood pasture has grown.

Wood pasture and the UK Biodiversity Action Plan

Wood pasture and parkland are the subject of a Habitat Action Plan led by English Nature (SNH's counterpart agency in England) as part of the UK Biodiversity Action Plan. Scottish Natural Heritage will maintain an inventory of ancient wood pasture sites in Scotland, with information from old maps and estate records helping to supplement biological and archaeological field surveys in providing evidence of a wood pasture history.

Wood pasture is a distinct habitat because of its historic management but the structure can be found imposed on a range of natural woodland, grassland and heathland communities, many of which are priority habitats in their own right. The woodland Habitat Action Plans (HAPs), for example,

include upland oakwoods, native pinewoods, upland ashwoods (with hazel or elm), upland birchwoods, lowland mixed broadleaves and wet woods. Each of these, together with slope alderwoods and areas of hawthorn and juniper, can contribute to wood pasture.

The semi-natural grassland or heath surrounding the trees can also be a priority for conservation. Wood pastures are grazing-maintained habitats, so looking after them will require appropriate management of the pasture.

Grassland benefits from a level of grazing that keeps the sward open and free of excess litter, and that creates gaps in which seedlings can establish. Too little grazing leads to a sward choked with long grass and uneaten litter, where plants cannot find space to regenerate. Excessive grazing, on the other hand, can eliminate variety and create short, species-poor swards, large areas of bare earth and invasions of thistles, docks or ragwort.

The ideal grassland for a wide range of plants, invertebrates, birds and mammals will contain a range of heights and structures, from short open swards with patches of bare soil to tussocks of tall grass and flowers.

Many species are associated with wood pasture, and Species Action Plans have been drawn up for some of the rarer ones.

Surviving wood pasture at Glen Finglas, a remnant of a historic royal hunting forest

14

Species groups associated with wood pasture in Scotland

Lichens

Lichens particularly enjoy the long continuity of veteran tree habitats, some key sites hosting well over 100 different species. Typical old-growth lichens include a number with Species Action Plans such as *Bacidia incompta*, *Opegrapha fumosa*, *Schismatomma graphidiodes* and the orange-fruited elm lichen *Caloplaca luteoalba*.

Bryophytes and ferns

Bryophytes (liverworts and mosses) similarly value continuity of habitat, and generally develop best in more shaded areas within well-developed canopies of mature trees. Epiphytic mosses, along with ferns such as common polypody, are a regular feature of veteran trees where, over time, moist organic matter can build up in forks, crevices and on wide branches. The blunt-leaved bristle moss, *Orthotrichum obtusifolium*, has its own Species Action Plan.

Saproxylic insects

Veteran trees are noted for the amazing diversity of niche habitats they provide for insects that live or feed on dead and decaying sapwood. Wet micro-habitats such as sap-runs, rot-holes, water pockets, decaying sap and wet decaying sapwood tend to be favoured by saproxylic flies, which possess sucking mouthparts. Beetles have chewing mouthparts and tend to prefer dry deadwood, decaying heartwood and bark. Both groups can be highly specific to particular niches and require different habitats for different stages in their life cycle. Micro-habitat requirements are usually more important than the species of host tree, although some insects do show a preference. They include the Red Data Book *Hammerschmidtia* hoverflies, which are associated exclusively with aspen, and the bark/ambrosia beetle, *Dryocoetinus villosus,* which is normally found only on oak, beech and chestnut.

Fungi

A huge diversity of rare and threatened fungi are associated with ancient wood pasture: some 400 species are associated with ancient woodland and wood pasture. The fungi include the wood-rotting fungi in the trees, the *mycorrhizae* in the roots and the grassland fungi (such as waxcaps) which are found in unimproved pasture.

Butterflies and moths

Wood pasture is good for many species of *Lepidoptera* including the chequered skipper and the pearl-bordered fritillary, which depend on lightly grazed groundflora and the shelter and structure provided by open woodland conditions.

Birds

Threatened species such as the wryneck, spotted flycatcher, song thrush and tree sparrow are known to prefer open, grazed woodlands, and woodpeckers are attracted to the insect life in the standing deadwood of veteran trees.

Bats

The pipistrelle bat is a key predator in wood pasture, attracted by the range of flying insects and the roosting opportunities in hollow and large-canopy trees.

Vascular plants

Unimproved wood pasture provides a range of habitats for groundflora, sometimes retaining woodland herb species such as bluebell and dog's mercury within a grazing maintained grassland.

Mammals

Alongside the pipistrelle bat, the mix of open ground and wooded shelter provides excellent habitat for stoats, weasels, badgers, wildcats and foxes.

Top left: *Caloplaca luteoalba* - the orange-fruited elm lichen
Top right: *Ctesias Serra*
Bottom left: *Carterocephalus palaemon* - chequered skipper butterfly
Bottom right: *Pipistrellus pipistrellus* - pipistrelle bat

Diagram to show an ideal veteran tree site for wildlife

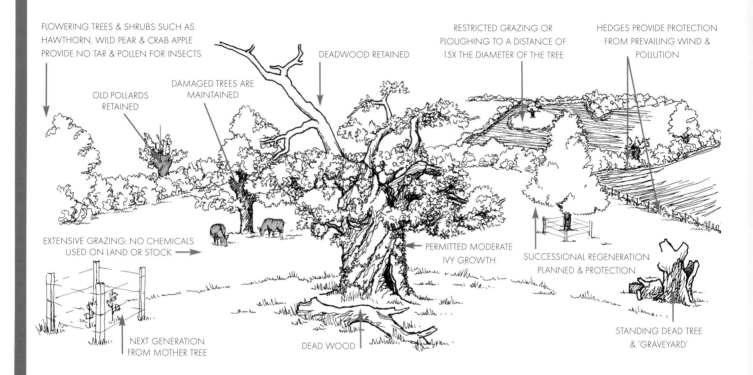

FLOWERING TREES & SHRUBS SUCH AS
HAWTHORN, WILD PEAR & CRAB APPLE
PROVIDE NO TAR & POLLEN FOR INSECTS

OLD POLLARDS
RETAINED

DAMAGED TREES ARE
MAINTAINED

DEADWOOD RETAINED

RESTRICTED GRAZING OR
PLOUGHING TO A DISTANCE OF
15X THE DIAMETER OF THE TREE

HEDGES PROVIDE PROTECTION
FROM PREVAILING WIND &
POLLUTION

EXTENSIVE GRAZING: NO CHEMICALS
USED ON LAND OR STOCK

PERMITTED MODERATE
IVY GROWTH

SUCCESSIONAL REGENERATION
PLANNED & PROTECTION

NEXT GENERATION
FROM MOTHER TREE

DEAD WOOD

STANDING DEAD TREE
& 'GRAVEYARD'

Veteran trees in a wood pasture tend to be open grown and unshaded. Because of their age, structure and deadwood component they play host to a range of other species. The long undisturbed conditions in the trees allow 'old-growth' species and communities to develop.

Smaller tree species such as hawthorn, blackthorn, rowan and elder may themselves be veterans, but will also occur in patches of regeneration or in hedges. These provide nectar sources in early spring for the specialist deadwood insects and habitat for birds and other predators.

A ripe old age

Old orchards bear many similarities to wood pasture. The trees were regularly pruned, propped up and kept alive, and they were often grazed by sheep and geese. Where they remain untended, the veteran fruit trees host old-growth lichens, fungi and dead wood habitat. The groundflora can be rich semi-natural grassland, and the blossom and fallen fruit provide a ready supply of food for insects. Many have been lost since the Second World War, but interest in old orchards is burgeoning as a source of traditional fruit varieties. Often these are preserved by grafting cuttings onto new rootstocks. However, keeping the old trees alive and managing them in such a way as to conserve their biodiversity would prove very beneficial for wildlife.

Above. an old apple orchard on the Isle of Eigg where the veteran fruit trees host interesting 'old-growth' lichens

Right: The main lichen species on this old apple tree is *Lobaria pulmonaria* - lungwort

A valued landscape

The effect of broad, spreading trees scattered over grassland has long been recognised as a classically attractive landscape. Some think this is an innate recognition dating back to when our ancestors ranged the African savannahs (and Scottish wildwood). Over the centuries, landscape architects and designers have successfully applied the formula in both naturalistic and more formal styles for appreciative landowners. Today, the wood pasture structure is echoed in city and country parks, in golf courses (which not uncommonly occur on former wood pasture sites) and in gardens, picnic sites and suburban landscaping. References to wood pasture scenery can be found in much visual imagery - in old portraits of landowning families, children's TV programmes, or in corporate advertising - suggesting qualities of peacefulness, security, maturity and permanence.

Areas of wood pasture make for beautiful scenery when viewed from a distance. At close range the trees themselves provide beauty, shade, scale, timelessness and seasonal change. Naturally, such sites are ideal for recreation.

Wood pasture at Glen Finglas

Dalkeith Old Wood

Dalkeith Old Wood, on Buccleuch Estates near Edinburgh, is an exceptional example of Scottish wood pasture. Possibly starting life in the twelfth century as a royal hunting forest, and bounded by walls and rivers, it remains today an astonishing place. Acres of grazed pasture set with hundreds of ancient oaks, mostly multi-stemmed with here only a few of them pollarded, it creates a vision of serenity and beauty. It is designated as a Site of Special Scientific Interest; and cattle still range beneath the trees as they have done for centuries. Both Dalkeith Old Wood and the Cadzow oaks at Hamilton High Park are key sites for rare saproxylic beetles and lichens.

Top left and right: veteran oaks in Dalkeith Old Wood

Bottom left: *Phymatodes testaceus* - saproxylic longhorn beetle - an indicator of ancient woodland

The Nest

The Nest is a small ash-elm wood running along a steep south-facing slope overlooking the River Tweed. A scattering of veteran ash trees skirts the top of the wood, below which a stand of ash has regenerated over an ageing understorey of hazel, hawthorn, blackthorn, elder and holly. At one end, on a gentler slope, there are the remains of some big open-grown elms which have finally succumbed to Dutch elm disease. The wood has always been grazed, and calcareous grassland forms a wide glade in the centre peppered with primrose, rock rose and scattered hawthorn bushes.

There are a few woods like this on the south-facing slopes of the Tweed Valley with open-grown veteran trees, a grassland flora and pockets of tree regeneration in patches of thorn and on rockier sites. The Scottish Borders have long been sheep and cattle country. It is quite possible that, in the past, wood pasture like this was much more evident as a belt of sheltered grazing between the floodplain meadows and the higher, exposed moorland.

Top: veteran ash tree in wood pasture at The Nest

Bottom left and right: rock rose and primrose: species associated with grassland grow in the open wood pasture at this site

Rassal Ashwood National Nature Reserve

Rassal Ashwood grows on a rare outcrop of limestone in Wester Ross. It is the most northerly ashwood in Britain, and was designated a National Nature Reserve in 1956 for the hundreds of old ash trees and their uniquely valuable lichen flora. The site was being grazed, so over the years fenced exclosures were put up allowing regeneration of ash, hazel, rowan and willow. Some areas were planted with native species to speed up the process.

Early farmers did not ignore this relatively fertile site. There are signs of past cultivation in the small, stone-cleared terraces set within wide stone walls. They cultivated crops where the soil was deepest, and may have enhanced soil fertility by manuring. They clearly controlled the grazing, allowing the trees to regenerate on the rockier sites where cultivation was not possible. The ash trees would have been valued probably for leaf fodder, and certainly for poles and tools, as well as shelter for stock.

Rassal seems to be a historic wood pasture. Sites similar to Rassal are found in Scandinavia, and it may be that the structure dates back to the Viking era. It is now being suggested that, in at least part of the site, the regenerating trees are thinned out and cleared from the more obvious terraces to create open glades. These will require seasonal grazing. The plan would be to retain the character of the site and allow the stock of open-grown veteran trees with their rich oceanic lichen flora to be maintained.

Rassal is also a living example of 'biocultural heritage', a term used in Europe to describe features such as the old ash trees at Rassal, which have unique biological values (for example, as a habitat for rare epiphytic lichens) yet are themselves partly a product of man's interaction with this land over the centuries.

Top: veteran ash trees growing on the rocky outcrops and boulder cairns at Rassal. Middle: with the exclusion of grazing hazel is now regenerating onto the stone-cleared terraces at Rassal which early farmers would have cultivated. Bottom: *Hygrocybe punicea* occurs in the grazed grassland adjacent to Rassal

Glen Finglas

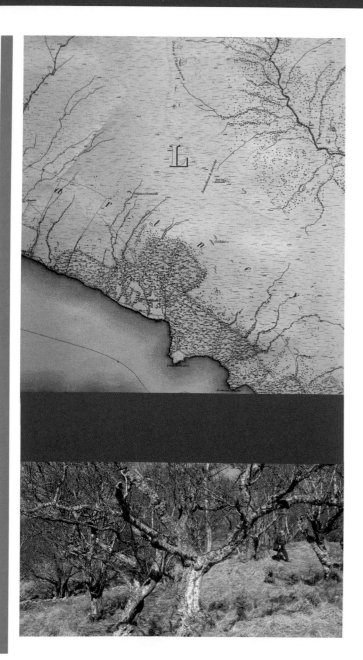

In 1996 the Woodland Trust purchased Glen Finglas estate, near Brig o' Turk on the eastern edge of the Trossachs. The site includes about 47 hectares of remnant wood pasture scattered over approximately 500 hectares within Glens Finglas and Meann. This was formerly a royal hunting forest frequented by the Stewart kings and actively managed for game, livestock and woodland. There are the ruins of several small homes up the glen and the patterns of previous cultivation can still be seen close by.

Over the last couple of centuries, livestock farming has been the main land use, with the woodland cover reduced to a scatter of veteran alder, hazel, birch and ash. Many appear to show evidence of past pollarding and coppicing. Some have survived by suckering, or layering of drooping branches, allowing individual trees to achieve a great age and for old-growth lichens and fungi to develop.

The Woodland Trust is regenerating native woodland on much of the surrounding glen but the open ground and ancient wood pasture areas will continue to be lightly grazed by deer and by their own flock of 1,800 sheep and 60 Luing cattle. Regeneration and suckering around the veterans will be controlled where it threatens to shade out the lichens and the grazing will be fine-tuned to re-create a landscape of open woodland and glades.

Glen Finglas has been popular for recreation since the Victorian era and the Woodland Trust is maintaining a number of walks, cycle routes and hill tracks with picnic facilities and interpretation of the landscape features. Over time they hope to create a place where farming, deer, recreation and wildlife conservation can co-exist in a mutually beneficial way.

Top: excerpt of the 1860 OS map of the Glen Finglas showing how extensive the wood pasture at this site once was

Bottom: hazel 'pollards' at Glen Finglas. The natural growth form of hazel is multi-stemmed; single-stemmed hazels such as these develop as a result of deliberate management and subsequent grazing, which prevents the growth of the new shoots

Present-day threats

The wood pasture that remains today has survived at least a century or two of neglect. Increasingly, time will count against this habitat as the trees reach the final stages of decay and death. Every wood pasture site that is lost depletes the remaining resource, rendering it more fragmented and isolated. This may have serious consequences for the rare species which depend upon it. A number of present-day activities are hastening the demise of wood pasture.

Agriculture

Many veteran trees and semi-natural grasslands have been lost in recent years to agricultural development through field enlargement and pasture 'improvement'. Applying inorganic fertilisers or lime to grassland communities causes a reduction in the range of species. It also makes the grass compete more strongly with the trees for water and other nutrients and affects the mycorrhizal fungi on tree roots. Even manure spreading may stress veteran trees by nitrogen enrichment; and if stock are given feed supplements this can have the same effect. Applications of herbicides, fungicides and insecticides, either deliberately, or indirectly by drift and drainage, can seriously damage veteran trees and their associated species. There is some concern over the use of broad-spectrum anti-parasite medications used to control worms and insects in sheep and cattle. These can remain active in animals' droppings, delaying their breakdown and affecting populations of invertebrates associated with dung. Animals naturally congregate under trees for shade or shelter, where a build-up of dung or pesticides can exacerbate the impact on the trees and the specialist flora and fauna.

Anoplotrupes stercorosus - the Northern Dumbledor Beetle - on cow dung. Insects such as this beetle are part of the natural cycling of nutrients in grassland and wood pasture

Left: a veteran oak tree previously growing in an open wood pasture has been underplanted with non-native conifers. As they grow these young trees shade out the old veterans, which eventually succumb and die

Below: A superb example of a veteran sweet chestnut at Rosslyn Glen now competing for light with the young ash and sycamore which have regenerated under its canopy

Forestry

Afforestation with exotic conifers over the last century has made serious inroads into the upland wood pasture resource. Wood pasture landscapes, having lost their historic utility, were prime targets for plantation forestry, and big old broadleaved trees were often ring-barked before areas were planted. Sites afforested in the major expansion decades of the 1970s and 1980s are now reaching a crucial stage. The plantation trees are shading out the remaining veterans, the remnant groundflora and the lichens and bryophytes on the stems. These features will not survive unless action is taken to gradually open up the canopy. Forestry continues to be a threat. Normally tree cover below 20% is not classed as woodland, so areas of wood pasture could still attract grants for planting with exotic conifers or the regeneration of native woodland. A wider recognition of wood pasture habitat and its values is vital if remaining sites are to be safeguarded and threatened sites restored.

A future for wood pastures

The future for wood pasture requires long-term vision. The habitat was created over centuries and will need continued management for centuries to come. The existing Habitat Action Plan for Wood Pasture and Parkland is already in progress, identifying actions and resources for maintenance and restoration, particularly sites threatened by underplanted trees. The plan also proposes the creation of new sites suitably situated to reduce the fragmentation of the habitat and to ensure that there are replacement veteran trees to maintain the flora and fauna.

Amenity and recreation areas

Wood pastures make excellent amenity and recreation sites. However, trees, and veteran trees in particular, can be damaged by trampling, vandalism, fires, car parking or the construction of ditches and paths. There is also a tendency to keep parks 'tidy' and that often means cutting off and removing deadwood, mowing and applying herbicide around trees and fertilising grass - all of which reduce biodiversity. Where veteran trees and dead standing trees are present alongside roads, access routes and visitor sites, safety and accident liability considerations will play a part in their loss.

Well-intentioned management

Landowners may see what they regard as an untidy and derelict tree and have it removed to replace it with a tidy group of young trees. Archaeologists might want to remove trees from an ancient site, not realising that the trees themselves may be fully old enough to be considered as historic landscape features and perhaps even rarer than the site beneath. Again, as discussed at Rassal Ashwood above, veteran trees can be seen as examples of 'biocultural heritage'. That means that compromise solutions to their management may be required, such as pollarding rather than felling a veteran tree with rare lichens which is growing on an ancient monument.

Top: Some members of the Natural History Society of Glasgow photographed on an excursion to Cadzow Forest, Hamilton, 25th September 1885. This site has changed very little in over 100 years

Bottom: a view of Cadzow today. Young oaks grown from acorns collected from the old trees have been planted in some of the open areas to grow into the 'veterans of the future', thus ensuring continuity of the habitat

To provide wildlife habitat

The specialist species associated with veteran trees already receive limited protection in parklands designated as Sites of Special Scientific Interest. However, there is considerable scope for restoration and management of the many undesignated wood pasture remnants which would provide additional wildlife benefits. Important species under threat, such as the black grouse and red squirrel, would benefit from wood pasture conditions.

Expanding or creating new wood pastures is an option, although the biodiversity benefits would be less direct, as we cannot create instant veteran trees. New wood pasture would however provide a useful linkage in the development of habitat networks. SNH and the Forestry Commission are promoting the network concept to reduce the fragmentation of native woodland and encourage transitions to other habitats. Wood pasture provides a relatively porous semi-natural habitat, enabling populations of both open-ground and woodland wildlife to extend across 'stepping stones' of suitable cover.

Top left: species such as the Black Grouse would benefit from the restoration and expansion of wood pasture

Top right: grazing animals, whether domesticated livestock or wild deer, are needed to maintain the characteristic structure of a wood pasture

Opposite page: wood pasture can provide an important stepping stone in the landscape linking woodland and open-ground habitats

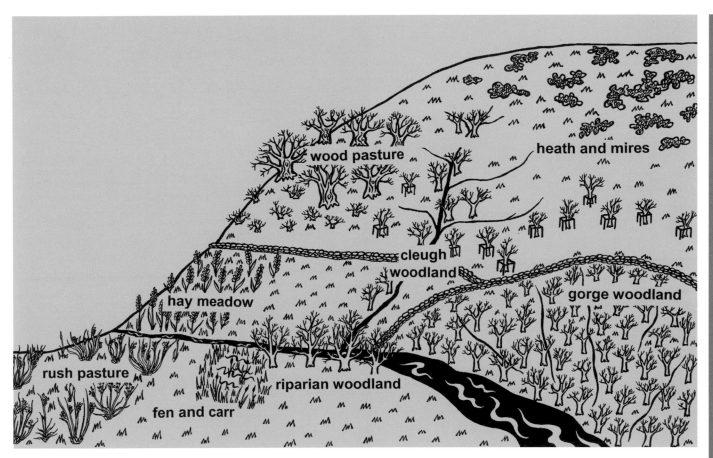

Habitat Networks

The labels within the illustration read:

- wood pasture
- heath and mires
- cleugh woodland
- gorge woodland
- hay meadow
- rush pasture
- riparian woodland
- fen and carr

To promote an attractive cultural landscape

Open-grown trees and small patches of open woodland provide for
wildlife and shelter, but also add to the attractiveness of the landscape.
Plantation forestry can be controversial where it blocks views and
significantly alters landscapes. It is often the large vistas and exposed
topography that distinguish the Scottish landscape and attract our visitors.
Wood pasture, however, is a historic cultural land use, which may provide
a more acceptable approach to increasing tree cover in sensitive areas,
while maintaining views along the valleys and access to the hills.

Cattle grazing the wood pasture of Glen Finglas

To enable demonstration and interpretation of historic land uses

The land-use history of Scotland is an important part of our cultural heritage and provides links to the lives and work of previous generations. Much apparent evidence of that history, together with its craft and folklore, has been erased by two centuries of agricultural improvement. It might be appropriate to re-create a few examples of working wood pasture, demonstrating previous farming practices and traditional breeds of cattle, sheep and goats, alongside pollarding, haymaking and woodcraft.

To contribute to sustainable land use in the uplands

Wood pasture provided a sustainable sheltered grazing resource for centuries, while providing soil protection and maintaining wildlife and game species. Today much of the Scottish uplands are overgrazed by deer and sheep, preventing the re-establishment of native trees. Where forests are created they usually exclude livestock, quickly alter habitats and replace the farming landscape.

Wood pasture may offer a structure that can reunite forester, farmer and naturalist in restoring and maintaining a valued habitat and a sustainable multiple land use. The Scottish Agricultural College at Kirkton Farm near Crianlarich is testing methods to establish trees within grazed land. Such trials may suggest ways to restore and create new wood pasture on the open hill without displacing the livestock. Wood pasture is less likely to confront landscape, sporting and access concerns than closed forest and could, indeed, benefit them all.

What does restoration involve?

Top and middle: gradual opening up of the canopy around infilled veteran trees

Bottom: once restoration of the trees is completed, grazing should be intoduced to allow a grassy sward to develop and prevent this reverting to scrub

Wood pasture sites are clearly threatened in a number of different ways, but steps for restoration and maintenance are, in theory at least, fairly straightforward. However, where field survey identifies rare or important species specialist advice should be sought to ensure that any proposed restoration is appropriate. As in all dealings with veteran trees, changes to their surroundings should be done gradually.

Where underplanted or naturally regenerating trees are shading out the veteran trees the canopy needs to be gently opened up to re-expose them to sunlight. In broadleaved stands the understorey could be maintained as coppice while allowing new standards to grow to replace the veteran resource. In more recent plantations, where elements of the existing groundflora remain, the understorey trees should be gradually removed to re-create linked areas of open ground around the veteran trees.

Overgrazed sites will often first require a reduction of wild deer numbers to maintained low levels. Grazing by domestic stock should be deliberately managed to establish and refine a regime that enables scattered trees or patches of regeneration to develop. Cattle tend to be preferred to sheep in promoting tree regeneration, and stock farmed organically can reduce the risk to biodiversity from agro-chemicals and animal medicines.

The semi-natural ground flora is a key element of wood pasture but, in lowland sites in particular, the sward has often been improved by spreading lime or fertilisers, reducing the species diversity. If these practices cease, it will slowly start to revert to a more natural pasture. Nutrient stripping is possible by taking repeated hay cuts, and re-seeding would speed the re-establishment of species-rich grassland communities.

In a few cases, a lack of grazing may be allowing the pasture to become rank, and grazing should be re-introduced to maintain the pasture species.

In the absence of grazing, hazel regenerates well and will revert to its characteristic multi-stemmed growth form

Restoration will take time and there may be circumstances where it makes sense to intervene to maintain veterans and hasten the regeneration of replacements. If veteran trees are very advanced and sparse, small stock exclosures could be used to encourage light regeneration close by. The planting of seedlings, protected by shelters, may be necessary if seed of appropriate species is not being produced. Deliberate layering of branches or protection of suckering could revitalise existing trees, maintaining the root system and its associated flora and fauna.

Experiments with tree surgery and gentle re-pollarding may offer ways to prolong the life of veterans, while young trees can be pollarded to encourage early development of characteristics associated with veteran trees.

If the trees have been pollarded in the past, it would be interesting from a historical perspective to continue this practice in some sites.   However, pollarding needs to be repeated every few years. It is skilled, difficult work, and expensive if there is no useful output (apart from the restoration of a historic landscape). Re-pollarding long-neglected veterans is probably not a good idea, unless there is good reason to believe it will benefit the trees and there are plenty on which to experiment. It would be easier to pollard young and existing 'middle-aged' trees to create a range of age classes.

Careful pollarding of a veteran ash multi-stemmed tree which overhangs a medieval graveyard near Loch Sween in Knapdale Forest. Forestry Commision staff are pollarding the tree to preserve the biological and cultural values of the old tree, while also protecting the carved gravestones from possible damage if the tree ever fell or uprooted

Veteran ash pollard

Have a stake in wood pasture

So far attention to wood pasture in Scotland has been limited to land-use historians, naturalists, conservation bodies, the government agencies and a handful of interested individuals and enlightened landowners to whom we are indebted.

Work by Scottish Natural Heritage to develop the inventory of existing sites helps to increase our knowledge of the habitat and draw it to the attention of the owners of remnant ancient wood pasture. Some are on public land: in forests, country parks and nature reserves. Government agencies and local authorities can lead the way in establishing best practice for restoration and management.

Financial incentives under the Rural Development Regulation can encourage estate owners, farmers and conservation organisations to restore and expand priority sites for biodiversity conservation. Local communities throughout Britain have already been active, particularly in the restoration of old orchards and in conserving parklands. Community woodland groups in Scotland could play a part in conserving wood pasture, combining biodiversity objectives with opportunities for local recreation and environmental improvement.

The development of new wood pastures as a sustainable multipurpose land use will require the continued input of research organisations such as the Scottish Agricultural College and The Forestry Commission's Forest Research Agency. Above all, however, it will need the interest and co-operation of innovative landowners who are willing to put theory and research into practice, marrying the benefits of trees and livestock farming. Both are vital to the long-term management of this aspect of the Scottish countryside.

Further reading

CCW (1997) *Orchards and Parkland Scheme Handbook*. Countryside Council for Wales

Denton, M.L., Godfrey, A., Hemingway, D.G., Skidmore, P. (2001). *Grassland Management Handbook*

Scottish Natural Heritage Commissioned Report BAT/LI02/99/00/48 (Unpublished report) Saproxylic Invertebrate Survey Hamilton High Parks SSSI 1999-2000.

Quelch, P. (2000) *Upland Pasture Woodlands in Scotland part I.* Scottish Forestry 54(4) pp 209-214

Quelch, P. (2001) *Ancient Wood Pasture in Scotland.* Millennium Award Scheme publication

Quelch, P. (2001) *Upland Pasture Woodlands in Scotland part II.* Scottish Forestry 55(2) pp 85-92

Read, H. (1999) *Veteran Trees: A Guide to Good Management.* Veteran Trees Initiative, English Nature

Rodger D, Stokes, J and Ogilvie, J (2003) *Heritage Trees of Scotland* (The Tree Council)

Rotheray, G. (1997) *The Conservation of Saproxylic Diptera in Scotland.* Scottish Natural Heritage Commissioned Report F96AC306 (Unpublished report)

Smith, M. and Holl, K. *Ancient Wood Pasture in Scotland: Classification, Inventory and Management.* Scottish Natural Heritage Research Survey and Monitoring Report No. F01AA108.

Smout, T.C. (ed) *People and Woods in Scotland: a History.* (Edinburgh University Press, 2003).

UK Biodiversity Group (1998) *Tranche 2 Action Plans,* Vol II. *Parkland and Wood Pasture Habitat Action Plan.* English Nature, Peterborough

Also in the Natural Heritage Management Series

A series of books, binders and leaflets addressing the wide range of issues facing natural heritage management today.

Car Parks in the Countryside:
A Practical Guide to Planning, Design and Construction

A guide to the planning, design, construction and management of small rural car parks in Scotland. Ideal for site managers, land owners, local authorities, funding agencies and local communities.
ISBN 1 85397 087 5   £9.99

Upland Pathwork:
Construction Standards for Scotland

A must for anyone involved in upland footpath management. The principles of footpath management, factors to be considered before starting any pathwork, practicalities of path construction and maintenance are all covered in this useful manual compiled by The Footpath Trust for the Path Industry Skills Group.
ISBN 1 85397 062 X   £15.00

Minerals and the Natural Heritage
in Scotland's Midland Valley

Minerals extraction has, arguably, the greatest range of impacts upon the natural heritage of any form of development. This book provides data and guidance with which to assess the sensitivity of different natural heritage interests to mineral development.
ISBN 1 85397 081 6   £9.99

A Technical Guide to the Design and
Construction of Lowland Recreation Routes

A handbook full of practical advice on the engineering elements of how to construct routes for walkers, cyclists and horse-riders on low ground in the countryside. With information on assessing the site and approaching construction – helping you to ensure that your path is safe, durable and a pleasure to use.
ISBN 1 85397 024 7 pbk 28pp £7.99

Field Guide to Upland Habitats:
Surveying Land Management Impacts

For decades there have been debates about the 'state' of the uplands and what is needed to improve them. Concern has focused especially on the impacts of high numbers of sheep and deer and on the occurrence of uncontrolled burning. In this two-volume guide SNH attempts to resolve some of these problems. The guide is aimed at professional field staff in the conservation agencies and non-governmental organisations, and ecological contractors undertaking field surveys.
ISBN 1 85397 296 7

£30.00 for Volumes I & II. Volumes not sold separately

Montane Scrub

Montane scrub, that fascinating mix of gnarled and twisted 'wee trees' and other plants and animals associated with them, is the 'Cinderella' habitat of Scotland. Without positive measures for reinstatement, the future for this valuable habitat looks bleak. Forming a natural zone between the treeline and the high montane heath, montane scrub adds diversity to the scenery, helps to prevent erosion, and provides a haven for nesting birds and a valuable food source for migrants.
This beautifully illustrated booklet outlines the steps the Montane Scrub Action Group is taking to restore Scotland's hills to their former glory.
ISBN 1 85397 103 0   £3.95

SNH Publications Order Form: Natural Heritage Management Series

Title	Price	Quantity
Car Parks in the Countryside: A Practical Guide to Planning, Design and Construction	£9.99	
Upland Pathwork: Construction Standards for Scotland	£15.00	
Minerals and the Natural Heritage in Scotland's Midland Valley	£9.99	
A Technical Guide to the Design and Construction of Lowland Recreation Routes	£7.99	
Field Guide to Upland Habitats: Surveying Land Management Impacts	£30.00	
Montane Scrub	£3.95	
Wood pasture	£4.95	

Postage and packaging: free of charge within the UK.

A standard charge of £2.95 will be applied to all orders from the EU.

Elsewhere a standard charge of £5.50 will apply.

Please complete in **BLOCK CAPITALS**

Name _____

Address _____

_____

_____

Post Code _____

Type of Credit Card   MasterCard ☐   VISA ☐

Name of card holder _____

Card Number ☐☐☐☐ ☐☐☐☐ ☐☐☐☐ ☐☐☐☐

Expiry Date ☐☐ ☐☐

Send order and cheque made payable to Scottish Natural Heritage to:

Scottish Natural Heritage, Design and Publications, Battleby, Redgorton, Perth PH1 3EW

E-mail: pubs@redgore.demon.co.uk www.snh.org.uk

Please add my name to the mailing list for the   SNH Magazine ☐

Publications Catalogue ☐